THE CHANGEABLE WORLD
OF THE OYSTER

THE CHANGEABLE WORLD OF THE OYSTER

Joseph J. Cook

Illustrated with photographs

DODD, MEAD & COMPANY · New York

To E. L. Mayo, teacher and poet

ACKNOWLEDGMENTS

The author particularly wishes to thank the following: Kate F. Urquhart, Inmont Corporation; George H. Vanderborgh, Jr., vice president and technical director of Long Island Oyster Farms; John T. Hughes, director, State Lobster Hatchery and Research Station, Massachusetts; The American Museum of Natural History, New York City; California Department of Fish and Game; Florida Board of Conservation; Louisiana Wild Life and Fisheries Commission; New York State Department of Environmental Conservation; United States Department of Commerce, National Marine Fisheries Service; Virginia Institute of Marine Science; the Washington State Department of Fisheries; and Jan Cook for the illustration on page 11 and the diagrams on pages 17 and 75.

ISBN 9-396-06847-2

Library of Congress Catalog Card Number: 73-7094
Printed in the United States of America

Contents

I. The Oyster

Oysters are invertebrates, or animals without backbones. These sea creatures belong to the Phylum (a scientific division of animals) mollusca, one of the largest, most diversified groups into which man has divided the animal kingdom. Mollusks (from the Latin meaning soft-bodied) usually have a hard shell protecting the body. However, some mollusks, like the octopus, squid, cuttlefish, and the less romantic garden slug, do not have this outer shell but instead have a remnant of it inside their bodies. Mollusks are divided into six major classes. Oysters, along with snails, limpets, mussels, cockles, and clams, belong to the class Bivalvia or Pelecypoda.

Oysters are members of the Ostreidae family. Their protective shell is divided into two halves, each of which is called a valve. Oysters are known as bivalves, meaning they have a two-valved shell. While most other bivalves have two muscles holding the valves together, the oyster has only one.

The left or lower valve is thicker and rounder than the right valve. Oysters lie on the left valve in sea water, in bays, coves, and estuaries, waiting for the currents

This natural oyster bed in Florida has grown vertically, resulting in overcrowding and exposure of the oysters to the sun at low tide. These conditions produce small oysters of no commercial value.

Florida Department of Natural Resources

to bring microscopic plant and animal life to them. Except in the early stages of their life, they are sedentary unless moved by outside forces.

The life span of an oyster averages about fifteen years if it is undisturbed. The average age of an oyster found in the market is usually two to five years.

The family Ostreidae is made up of three genera—*Ostrea, Crassostrea,* and *Pycnodonta.*

Ostrea oysters, named by the scientist Linnaeus in 1758, are fairly flat with the left valve shallow, not as deeply curved as in most oysters, and circular in shape with a rather smooth shell. These oysters prefer cool, clear water and a bottom that is sandy, not muddy. They are native mainly to the waters of Europe, the south coasts of Australia and New Zealand, and have been found in the cold waters of Iceland. A small species is to be found on the Pacific coast of North America from Alaska to California. Commercially unimportant *Ostrea* are also found in the southern waters of North Carolina, Florida, Louisiana, and other Gulf states. *Ostrea* are adversely affected by extremely cold winters, tides that expose them to the hot summer sun, and excessive rains that alter the salinity of the sea water.

Crassostrea, named by Sacco, another man of science, in 1897, are comprised of many species. These oysters have a deeply cupped left valve and an elongated, fairly rough and bumpy outer shell, and are by far the most numerous and commercially important today. They are hardy specimens able to combat great and sudden changes in salinity of the water, as well as excessive sediment, thus enabling them to live on moderately muddy beds where they can indulge their appetites in the rich supply

Examples of four species of oysters: lower left, *Crassostrea gigas*, Great Pacific; lower right, *Ostrea edulis*, European flat; upper left, *Ostrea lurida*, U.S. Pacific Coast; upper right, *Crassostrea virginica*, Eastern. Notice the circular growth ridges which determine the shape of the valves.

of food found in estuaries, creeks, and inlets. These oysters are capable of living in fresh water for part of the day while the tide is out. They keep their valves tightly closed until the tide slowly brings back the salty, brackish water.

Crassostrea thrive in moderately warm temperate and tropical seas, and are native to the Atlantic and Gulf Coast shores of the United States, as well as Portugal, Japan, India, Australia, and New Zealand.

Pycnodonta, named by Fischer van Waldheim in 1834, have large, heavy shells with the left valve not deeply cupped. They usually live in the saltiest of water, in fairly deep, open seas. *Pycnodonta* do not grow together in great numbers, forming beds, so that, although edible, they are too difficult to obtain in sufficient quantity to make them commercially important. The best known example is the *Pycnodonta hyotis*, which is found in most oceans, notably in coral reefs such as the Great Barrier Reef of Australia. Here the waters range from a few feet to depths of over three hundred feet. When the surface of the reef is exposed at extremely low tides, the mollusk may be found growing to great size, having zigzag shells weighing as much as seven pounds with a diameter or width of over eight inches.

It takes hundreds of thousands of oysters to make a healthy natural bed. The oysters are at the mercy of their environment—salinity and depth of water, temperature, food supply, the nature of the bottom beneath them, and predators. All these factors affect the oysters and make it possible for an experienced person to tell from the shape, the appearance of the shell, and, at times, the taste, from what area or bed an oyster came.

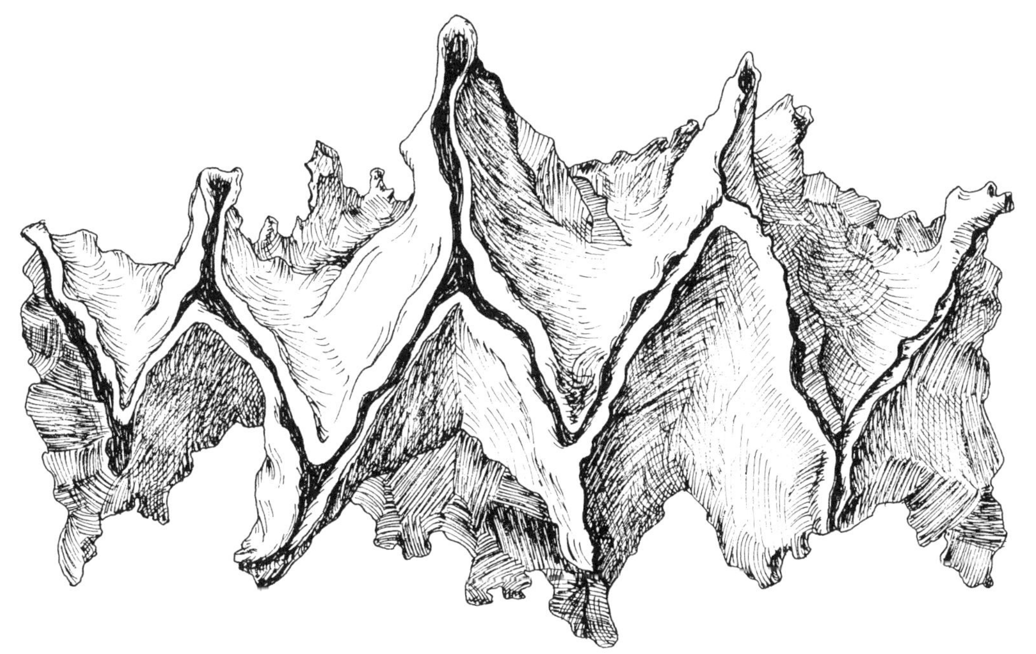

Pycnodonta hyotis, the largest of oysters, is a common inhabitant of coral reefs. The valves of the zigzag shell weigh as much as seven pounds, and may attain a diameter of over eight inches.

For centuries people who ate oysters looked for the precious pearl that was believed to be found in this mollusk. Even today, many people think that a pearl is formed within an oyster's valves. Some experts believe the idea originated with the early sea voyages to tropical waters in search of pearls, the pearl-producing mollusks mistakenly coming to be called pearl "oysters." Early English writers and poets, including Shelley and Swinburne, produced such passages as "He is a pearl within an oyster shell," and "Then love was the pearl of his oyster," which furthered the belief that oysters produce pearls.

Although an oyster, or any mollusk, irritated by some material within its shell, such as a speck of sand, may form an object resembling a pearl, it is not in reality a pearl. The chemical make-up of an oyster cannot produce the beauty and luster of a true pearl.

The so-called pearl "oyster," known as *Meleagrina margaritifera,* is related to the mussel. The inside of its valves is composed of an iridescent substance known as nacre, which gives luster to the pearl. This layer of glowing material is called mother-of-pearl and from it items of jewelry, buttons, and beads are made. Nacre is absent from the valves of edible oysters.

Relying on its salty environment for its very existence, the oyster has intrigued and nourished numerous civilizations since man first entered the sea in search of food.

2. What Makes an Oyster Tick?

The shell of an oyster completely surrounds the soft animal within and provides protection to it. During an oyster's life there are frequent and rather regular spurts of sudden growth which may add more than a quarter of an inch to the end or bill of the valves at a time. Growth takes place mainly in the spring and fall, stopping for a short period when the mollusk is reproducing in the warm months, and ceasing completely in the winter. Shell growth is also affected by the supply of food. Starvation stops it, while an abundant supply of food insures good growth.

As the shell grows, it is covered with a series of circular ridges. The final shape of the valves, which are unequal in size and differ in shape, depends on how the new growth is added. The left or lower valve is thicker and hollowed to accommodate the body, while the right or upper valve is flatter and thinner, like a lid. The valves are joined together at one end by a tough, elastic hinge-ligament. This ligament acts as a spring, allowing the valves to open.

The color of an oyster shell varies and is mainly a mixture of shades of brown,

A well-formed oyster shell indicates uncrowded
growing conditions and high-grade meat. At the
left of the top or right valve is the area where
the ligament or hinge connects it to the lower or
left valve. The dark, circular spot is where the
powerful adductor muscle is attached in an un-
opened oyster.

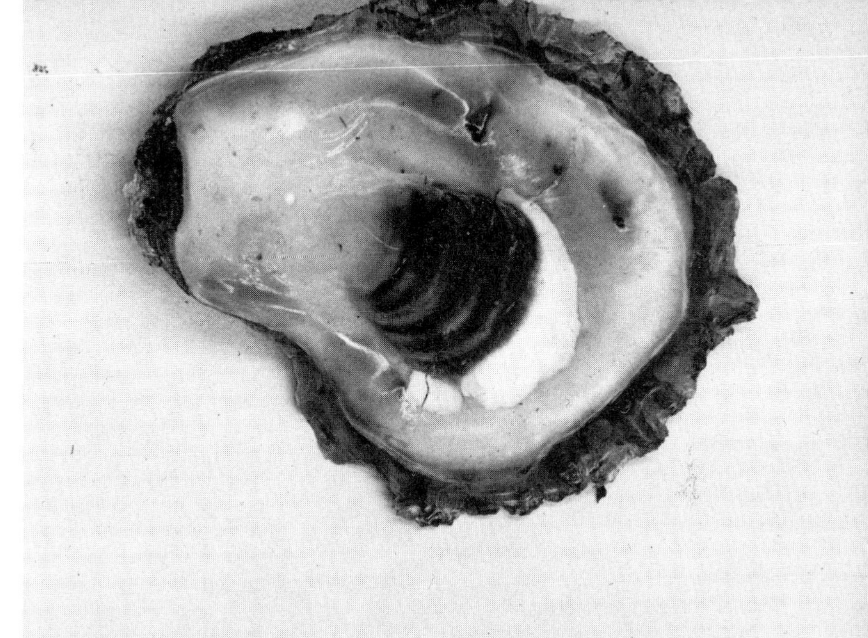

Florida Department of Natural Resources

gray, green, and white. Hard and rough in texture, the exterior is often bumpy and
uneven. The inside is a blend of gray and white, and is smooth.

An oyster shell serves as a home for other sea animals. Such creatures as sponges,
jellyfish, sea worms, sea spiders, and crustaceans ranging from microscopic specimens
to small crabs live their lives on the shell of an oyster. The majority of this marine
life neither gives nor takes anything from the oyster but uses the shell as we use
a floor in our house.

When the oyster is open, the adductor muscle is its most conspicuous organ. This
powerful muscle passes through the body and is attached to the inside front edges

Except for the oyster drill in the upper center, these sea creatures living on the
shell of an oyster are quite harmless.

Courtesy of the
Virginia Institute of Marine Science

of the valves and is the oyster's way of closing the valves and holding them shut. Scientists have observed that a force of twenty-five pounds is required to rip off the adductor muscle of an oyster. In an empty shell, dark, purplish spots remain where the adductor muscle touched it.

Lying on the more deeply cupped left valve is the headless, cream-colored living animal—the oyster. The parts of an oyster have been compared to the pages of a book by many scientific writers. First, a soft mass or body wall called the mantle which encloses the internal organs of the oyster is encountered. The mantle consists of three folds, or pages, shaped somewhat like plates.

The first fold draws in sea water through a series of glands which secrete a chalky substance known as calcium carbonate. This chemical, added in layers to the margin of the valves, does the work of forming the shell.

The middle fold houses two rows of tiny tentacles which are extremely sensitive. Any disturbance—a change in light made by a passing shadow or the presence of an irritating substance—is noted and causes a stimulus to pass through the nerves of the mantle to the adductor muscle, immediately closing the valves.

The inner fold of the mantle is the largest and most powerful of the three, controlling the inflow and outflow of water through the oyster.

Under the mantle lies an efficient gill system extending some two-thirds of the distance around the oyster's body. There are four gills, two half-gills on each side, which hang down from the roof or top of the mantle. They are extremely delicate, lined with great numbers of blood vessels, and covered with numerous fine hairs known as cilia. The cilia, when the valves are open in the water, are constantly in motion, seeking food and oxygen which are then strained by the gills. Scientists studying *Crassostrea* have noted that one oyster can pump more than a hundred gallons of water in one day!

Given an acre of oyster bed containing 100,000 to a million oysters, the water requirement for one day would be ten million gallons! Since such an enormous volume of water is necessary to supply food to an oyster bed, it becomes obvious that oysters can survive only in areas where a substantial flow of water occurs over the bed.

When an oyster's valves are parted, two distinct openings are present in the inner

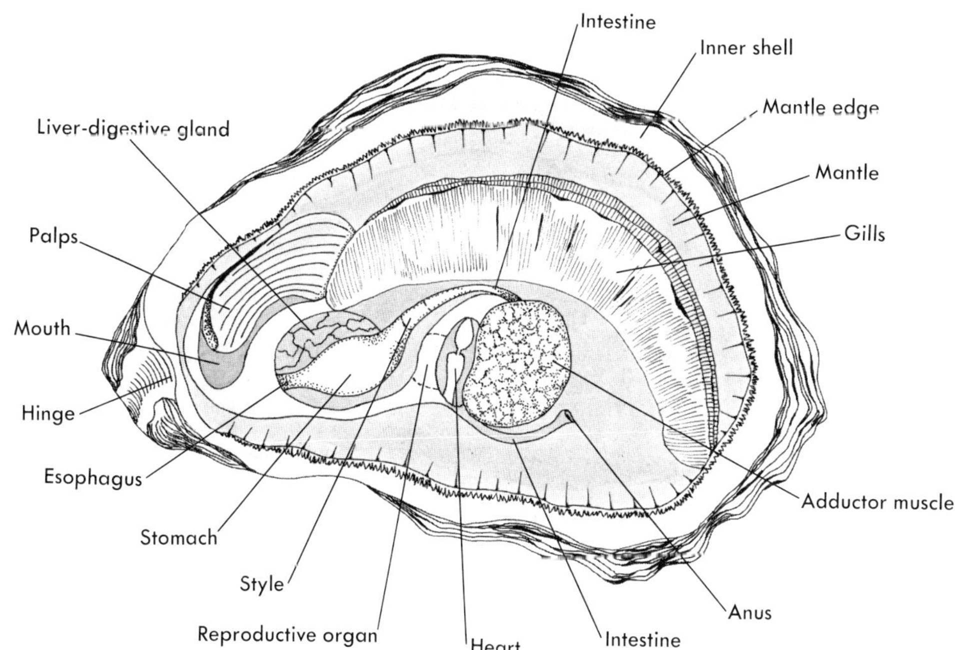

A partly dissected oyster in its left valve. The right valve and mantle have been removed to show important features of an oyster's anatomy.

Jan Cook

fold of the mantle. One serves as an inlet to the entering sea water, while the other serves an an outlet. As an oyster feeds, a thin sheet of mucus covers the gill surfaces. The microscopic food particles in the sea water, including larval forms of crustaceans or shellfish, fish, other sea animals, and plant life, collectively known as plankton, become entangled in the mucus and are "captured" by the oyster. The food is then pushed toward the inlet or mouth by the cilia. If the particles of food are indigestible they are violently shot out of the oyster by muscular tissue called palps. The acceptable plankton passes through the mouth and narrow gullet into the stomach. Here, an unusual process takes place. The majority of animals, including humans, digest their food first by secretion of juices, then assimilate or absorb the resulting liquid through cells lining the stomach. In the oyster, the process is just the opposite. Food is first absorbed and then digested.

The stomach and digestive glands of oysters are unique in the animal kingdom. Certain cells known as amoebocytes, similar to the white corpuscles of human blood, move freely about the oyster's digestive system, seeking out plankton and absorbing it into the walls of the glands to digest it.

Also in the stomach is a structure known as the crystalline style, a pliable rod about one-half an inch long. The cilia that line the style turn it continually, stirring the food. This action and the enzyme released by the style help in digestion. The crystalline style is not a permanent structure and dissolves after an oyster is removed from water since the animal is no longer feeding. Placed back in sea water, the mollusk resumes feeding and the rod reforms to carry on its digestive functions.

A short tube leads from the stomach into the intestine where waste and undigested material is passed to the anus. This waste matter is flushed away through the outlet by the current of water passing through the oyster.

The oyster breathes much as a fish does, using its fantastic gills and its mantle. The mantle is lined with many small, thin-walled blood vessels which extract the oxygen from the sea water and expel carbon dioxide. The colorless blood of the oyster, with its supply of oxygen, is pumped through all parts of the body by the animal's small, three-chambered heart which lies above the adductor muscle. Pulsation of the heart varies from fifteen to twenty-five beats per minute in warm water and decreases as water temperature drops. At water temperature of 40°F and below, respiration and heartbeat practically cease.

An oyster has a limited nervous system. It has two pairs of ganglia, which are a small collection of nerve-cell bodies and nerve tissue. As indicated, one pair of ganglia is located near the mouth and aids in selection of food. The other pair of ganglia, which is much more developed, is situated on the underside of the adductor muscle and aids in transmitting nerve impulses, "deciding" when the adductor muscle will close the valves.

The kidneys of the oyster are also located on the underside of the adductor muscle. They consist of a pair of porous tubes which flow into the mantle cavity above the gills. There the waste fluid passes from the small tubes and is carried away in the outgoing current.

The reproductive organ lies just above the heart. The sex of an oyster can be determined during the spawning season, when reproduction of young oysters is under-way, by microscopic examination of the gonad, the sex-cell producing organ. If sperm is present the oyster is male, while the presence of eggs establishes the fact that the mollusk is female.

It is in the area of sex that we shall see why the oyster may be called a "changeable" animal.

A parent oyster spawning in a laboratory. Note the milky fluid pouring from the right side of the bivalve.

3. A Changeable Creature

Pliny, the Roman naturalist, was familiar with oysters as were most people who lived along seacoasts from the earliest prehistoric days to the dawn of civilization. The oyster, probably due to its sedentary nature, easy accessibility, and food value, was undoubtedly studied longer and was better known than any other creature in the sea. However, it wasn't until the early 1880's that a Dutch scientist named Hoek discovered the changeable nature of the oyster's sex.

Oysters have the unusual ability to switch their sex, continually during the warm months in some species, or once during the year in the winter months in other species. This fascinating phenomenon is known scientifically as protandrie hermaphroditism, from *protos*, meaning first; *andros*, a man; Hermes, Greek god of travel; and Aphrodite, Greek goddess of love.

The change of sex is controlled by a number of environmental factors. The most important of these factors is nutrition. Huge amounts of plankton (microscopic plant and animal life) appear to encourage the female state in oysters, while lesser quantities of food result in male oysters. Furthermore, the sex organ of an oyster is to a large extent activated by water temperature, tide, and salinity of the water.

Reproduction does not, as was previously believed, stop the growth of a healthy oyster as long as food is plentiful. Spawning takes place during the warm months in any region and ceases as the water becomes colder.

The two most commercially valuable oysters, the *Ostrea* and the *Crassostrea,* as well as the less important *Pycnodonta,* go about their business of producing families in somewhat different fashions.

Ostrea oysters, known as larviparous because they lay their eggs inside their valves, produce a million eggs at a time. An *Ostrea* in the female state opens her valves during spawning and takes in sperm discharged by oysters in the male state. Fertilized and incubated, the eggs undergo initial development for a period of approximately seven days, and when the mother releases them into the water they are known as larvae.

Ostrea oysters change sex continuously throughout life. In cold waters they usually change once a year during the warm months. During the winter they become neutral. In warmer waters they may change repeatedly from male to female in a single season.

Crassostrea, the most common oyster in North America, and *Pycnodonta* are scientifically known as oviparous. These oysters cast their eggs into the water to be fertilized. A female *crassostrea* may discharge from 15 to 300 million eggs in one spawning. *Crassostrea* oysters usually start life as males and after the first year change to females. If they live long enough, they may revert back to males in their old age.

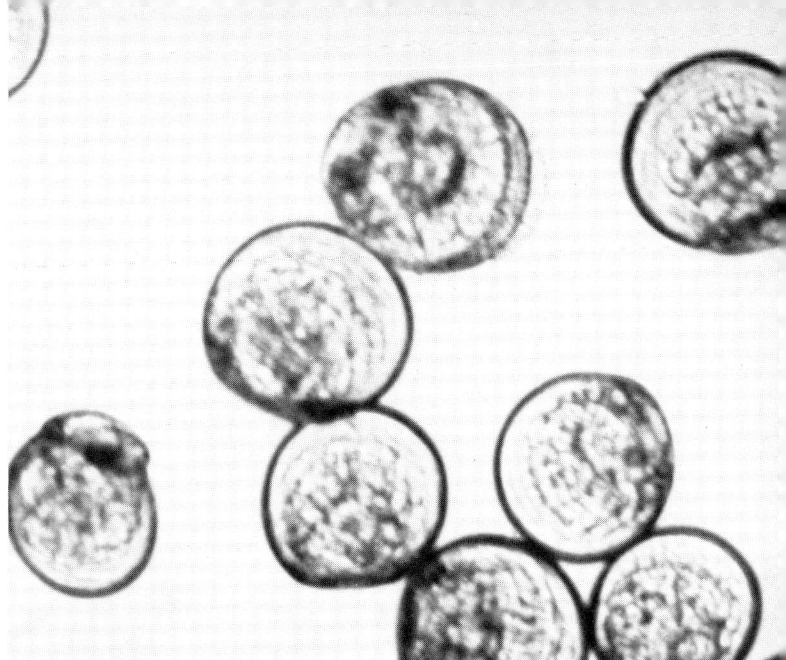

Oyster larvae as they appear when one week old, greatly magnified

Long Island Oyster Farms, Inc.

When they mate, the male *Crassostrea* oyster spawns first, releasing billions of sex cells into the surrounding water. The sperm, unlike the female's eggs, have the ability to swim and contain a chemical substance named diantlin. The presence of diantlin relaxes the adductor muscle of the female, causing her to spawn and release her cloudy mass of eggs into the sea water to be fertilized by the sperm. *Crassostrea* oysters may spawn several times during the warm months. Once a few individuals start spawning, the released sperm and eggs stimulate other oysters until great numbers in the bed are spawning at the same time.

Both eggs and sperm are microscopic in size and thousands upon thousands are eaten by plankton-feeding sea animals. Other factors such as pollution, adverse weather, temperature of the water, and currents continue to affect the oyster, so that even while reproducing it is at the mercy of the environment and man.

Millions of both male and female sex cells are released into the sea water to insure fertilization because it is a matter of such great chance. Unless the male and female sex cells unite within a short interval of a few hours, the eggs will disintegrate.

Whether the eggs and sperm unite within the oyster shell or in the open sea, the process of the embryo's development is the same. The embryo hatches into a larva and begins to form a pair of minute valves. At this stage the baby oyster is extremely small in size. About two hundred would cover the surface of a penny.

The free-swimming period for a tiny larva continues for approximately two weeks, aided by its swimming organ, the velum. A circular lobe projecting from between the two shells, the velum is fringed with the whisker-like cilia, which move the larva about while at the same time gathering food for it. When the cilia beat rapidly, the larva is propelled upward through the water. It then drifts slowly downward as the beating slows. The larva floats, up and down and about, sometimes covering a considerable distance. Less than one in ten survives the larval period, but the most precarious stage, settlement, is yet to come, when the chance for survival is approximately one in ten thousand.

After about two weeks, a tiny foot, which the oyster will soon utilize to settle on the floor of the sea, develops. The shell of the oyster has grown longer and heavier, and the young "spat," as the oyster is called during this stage, drops to the bottom,

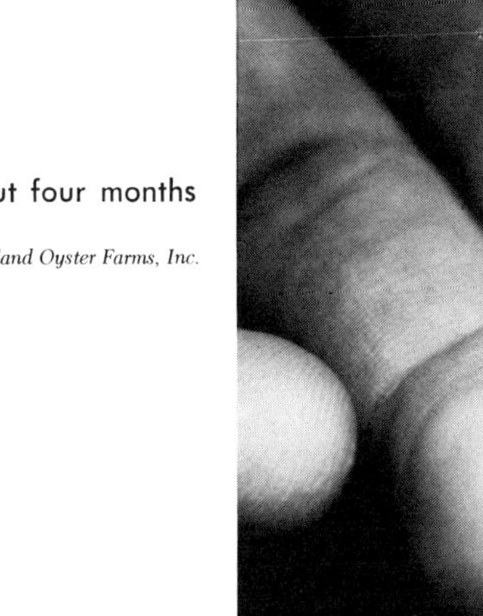
These tiny oysters are about four months old.

Long Island Oyster Farms, Inc.

where it tests objects with its new foot, seeking a suitable spot for attachment.

The act of attaching itself to a solid substance is known as "setting," "striking," or "spat fall." Should a hard surface be touched, the tiny foot grips it, the velum is withdrawn, and the spat explores the surface for a suitable place for a home. If the larva doesn't like the object after investigating, the foot is withdrawn, the velum extended, and "swimming" resumed. This may occur a number of times before the larva finds a satisfactory surface for attachment. C. M. Yonge, Professor of Zoology at the University of Glasgow and a leading authority on oysters, has stated that

Oyster larvae that "set" on a pier piling are so over-crowded and small that humans don't want them.
Florida Department Of Natural Resources

the larva settles "more readily on surfaces to which others are already attached." This may be nature's way of providing for the survival of oysters, through a better chance for reproduction.

If no suitable place for attachment is present, the spat may fall into oozy mud and die of suffocation. Because of lack of clean spots to settle, many billions of young oysters are lost in the bottoms of every bay, inlet, or bayou each year. Great numbers of these could be saved by the placement of dead oyster shells upon which they could strike.

Having found a clean surface on which to set, the spat attaches itself to the object by secreting a glue-like substance from a gland in its foot, and cements its left valve to the chosen object within a few minutes. The spat must succeed in its first attempt because the gland disappears immediately after depositing its sticky secretion. The oyster only has one chance. If it fails to set, it becomes part of the drifting plankton that is the food of fishes and other sea creatures.

Once an oyster is set, the foot and velum disappear and the oyster cannot move by itself ever again. Growth is rapid after attachment. Within two or three months of straining the sea for food, the spat may be as large as a dime, and within six to eight months it may be an inch or more in diameter. From this point in its development it is known as a seed oyster until it becomes marketable size. The average growth is approximately three inches during this period. At the end of the first year, sexual maturity is reached and the process of producing a new generation of oysters is started anew in the coves and estuaries of the sea.

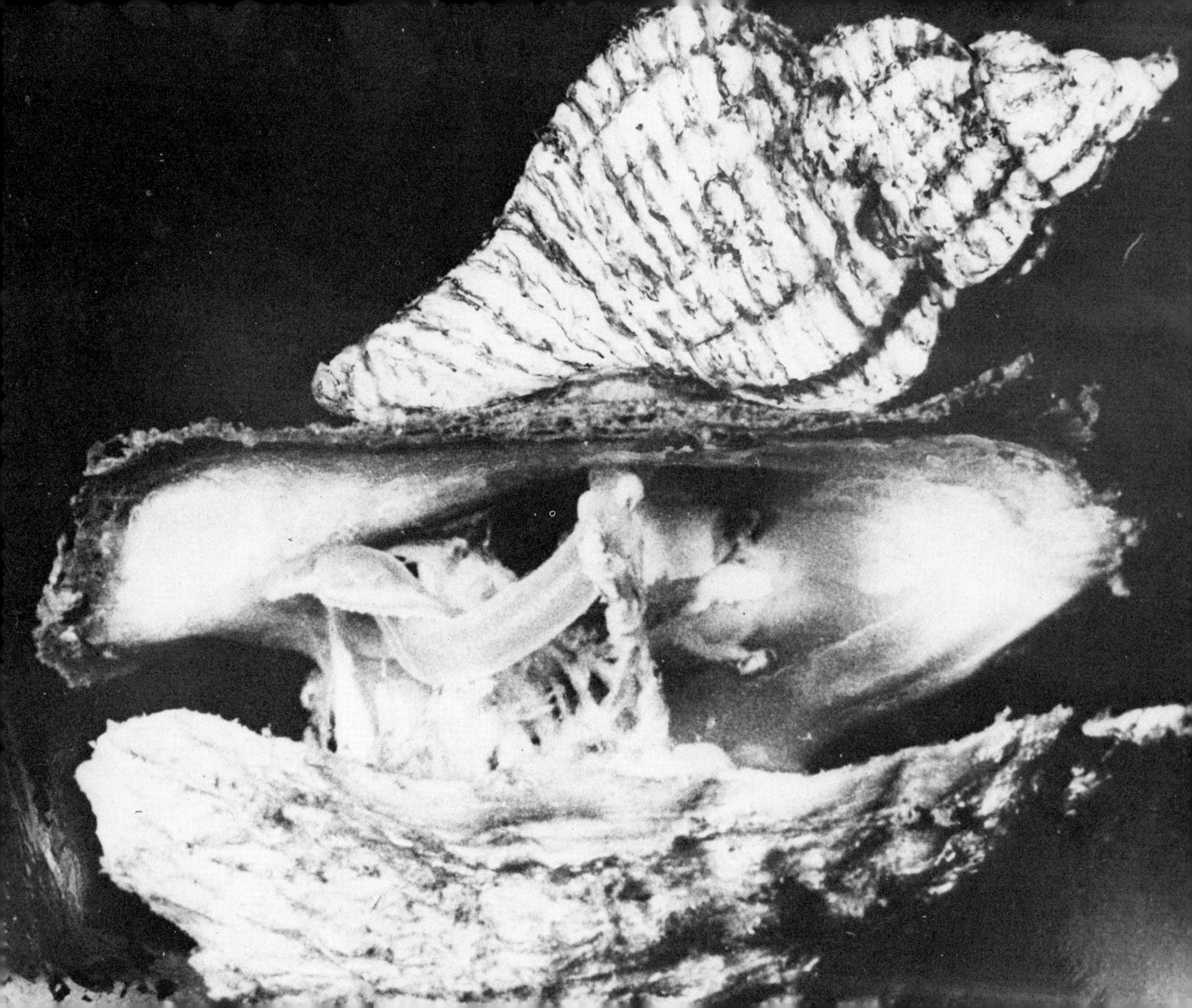

4. Predators, Diseases, and Environmental Factors

Even if oyster larvae escape innumerable obstacles and are successful in setting, they are still subject to onslaught by other sea creatures, parasitic diseases, and conditions affecting their habitat caused by nature and man. The oyster, lying on the floor of the sea with its sole protection the closing of its valves, has indeed a perilous and oftentimes nightmarish existence.

Drills, which are known also as boring snails or whelks, are undoubtedly the most dangerous sea enemy that the oyster must face. Housed in its small, coiled shell, this carnivorous univalve (one shell) is equipped with a long feeding tube known as the proboscis, at the end of which is a tongue with rows of tiny, horny teeth. Using its filelike tongue the drill bores a hole through the oyster shell, inserts the feeding tube, and consumes the meat of the oyster.

A deadly oyster drill that has successfully rasped a hole through the oyster's upper valve. Extending its feeding tube through the hole, it devours the body of the oyster.

Courtesy of the
Virginia Institute of Marine Science

In heavily infested areas, drills may demolish 100 per cent of the spat and thereby account for destruction of an entire set of oysters. However, drilling diminishes as the oyster ages and the shell thickens, so that large seed oysters planted in drill-infested regions have a good chance of surviving to market size.

The most destructive and widely distributed of all drills is known scientifically as *Urosalpinx* and comes from the eastern waters of the United States. This small marine snail, reaching lengths of from one to two inches, is commonly called the American oyster drill. This particular drill secretes a lime-dissolving chemical substance onto the oyster which hastens the operation of drilling through the shell. For many years, unknown to the oystermen shipping seed oysters from eastern waters to other oyster beds in the United States and to England, small drills were also included in the shipments. The British oyster industry has had to contend not only with a native drill, *Ocenebra* or sting winkle, but with the prolific American drill as well. The Pacific Coast oyster beds of the United States are menaced by a native species of drill, *Thais; Urosalpinx,* brought in years past with eastern seed oyster shipments; and a Japanese drill introduced with the early import of seed oysters from Japan.

Today, in an attempt to prevent further spread of drills and the transfer of other oyster enemies from one region or country to another, it is required that seed oysters be inspected for pests. Inspections carried out before shipments are made in order to avoid loss involved in transporting contaminated oysters.

In the warm waters of Florida, Louisiana, and other Gulf Coast states, the *Thais* drill is the cause of heavy oyster destruction. The popular name for *Thais*, in this locality, is conch (konk). Not to be confused with the true conch whose spiral shell is sometimes a foot long, *Thais* species grow to a length of only two inches. Since these small "conchs" must have water of high salinity, their attacks upon oyster beds occur during periods of drought when the fresh water supplies from nearby rivers and streams become extremely low. Then, in the salty water, these deadly predators overrun the oyster beds. A drill can bore a hole through the oyster's shell, or use its mouth parts to chip away small bits from the edges or bill of the oyster.

Due to the extensive damage done by these predators, trapping of "conchs" or drills is carried on by Gulf Coast oystermen. In the spring, when the drills are preparing to deposit their eggs, they tend to climb toward the surface. Taking advantage of this fact, the oystermen drive long poles into the drill-infested areas up which the snails crawl in order to lay their eggs. Workers pass by at intervals to pull the poles out of the water and scrape off both the drills and eggs into a container. Later they are destroyed.

Other methods of controlling drill invasion are the use of scuba divers, to hand pick them from oyster beds, and wire bags baited with young, thin-shelled oysters and placed about ten feet apart over the beds. These bags are fished regularly at intervals of about two weeks by lifting them into a boat and shaking the drills loose.

Drills have few known enemies and are extremely difficult for man to control. Since 1946, more than two thousand chemicals have been tested. While a few have been found effective on the predators, their use is not without risk of damage to

Hosing protecting chemical over oyster beds destroys drills.

U.S. Department of Commerce
National Marine Fisheries Service

the oysters themselves, as well as to other sea life. Extreme care must be used when applying pesticides to marine environments.

While these chemical controls on drills must be used with great caution, biological controls would eliminate the danger of polluting the water. Experiments have been made using a variety of shelled sea life as bait in drill-infested oyster beds. Studies show that *Urosalpinx* consumes thin-shelled mussels and barnacles before attacking oyster seed. Someday, possibly, drills will be diverted in this manner while young oysters gain time to thicken their shells. As indicated, later drill attacks would be less destructive because of the longer time required for drilling and feeding.

Another major enemy of the oyster is the starfish. These spiny creatures are not fish but animals that live in the sea and feast upon bivalves. Their flattened bodies

32

Scuba divers donning wet suits before entering the sea to check on the presence of two of the oyster's deadliest enemies — starfish and drills

Long Island Oyster Farms, Inc.

have a number of arms, usually five, extending outward like a star. Often starfish are a greater menace to oyster grounds than the drills, as even the thick-shelled, mature oyster can offer little resistance to them.

The rays or arms of a starfish radiate from the central body, with the mouth located on the bottom surface of this body. A groove extends from the mouth out to the tip of each of the arms, and there are rows of small holes in the grooves. The starfish can project slender tubes, known as tube-feet, from the grooves. Each of the minute feet has a sucker-like disk at the end.

A starfish attacks an oyster by wrapping its arms around the end of the mollusk, while its sucker-like feet exert a continuous pull to open the two halves of the shell. At one time it was believed that a starfish secreted a substance that paralyzed the oyster muscles and caused the valves to sag open. Laboratory experiments have determined, however, that the unrelenting pull by the starfish can cause the shells to separate about 1/25 of an inch.

At this slight separation of the oyster's valves, the starfish places its mouth on the opening. Then an astounding thing occurs. The starfish pushes its stomach inside out through its mouth and surrounds the soft flesh of the oyster. The oyster is digested right in its own shell by enzymes from the stomach wall of the starfish. After the stomach absorbs the digested animal, it is withdrawn through the mouth and back into its own body cavity. All that remains of the oyster are the empty valves as they lie on the bottom of the sea.

The five-armed starfish, known scientifically as *Asterias forbesi,* which grows to a diameter of twelve inches, causes millions of dollars worth of destruction yearly to the oyster beds in the northeast waters of the United States. Vast schools of the predators, numbering in the tens of thousands, swarm over oyster beds like an attacking army and devour the mollusks.

Formerly, in an attempt to control the starfish population, oystermen would chop quantities of the animals in half and dump them back in the water. It was unknown at the time that starfish have the power of regeneration, or the ability to grow new parts to replace parts they have lost. Consequently, each of the halves that had been returned to the water soon became a whole starfish! Instead of eliminating, the oystermen had increased the number of starfish.

Today there are a number of ways the oyster growers combat starfish, some of them by boat. In one case, a structure known as a tangle mop is dragged over the

Tangle mops with catch of the oyster's deadly enemy — the starfish
United Press International

oyster beds. The spines on adult starfish become entangled or caught in the dragging mops which, when brought on deck, are matted with thousands of the creatures. These are killed and later used as fertilizer. Another control from boats is by the use of suction dredges which work like giant vacuum cleaners on the sea's bottom, sucking up the lightweight starfish from the oyster beds.

A chemical, quicklime, is quite effective when it is spread over an oyster bed infested with starfish. The usual procedure is to apply the quicklime at low tide when the water is relatively calm. Then the chemical can settle where the oystermen want it. Rough water with strong currents can carry quicklime away from the beds. These applications kill the starfish but do not harm the oysters. Some lobstermen as well as other crustacean fishermen, however, believe it affects their catch.

One of the most interesting and romantic-sounding ways to control starfish is by scuba diving. Since starfish are always on the move, divers must frequently check the beds to remove the predators. Many oyster companies employ the divers on a yearly basis to keep the beds clear. In some sections of the United States, days are set aside, especially during the summer months, when professional and amateur scuba divers alike enter the waters to see how many starfish they can remove from the bedded areas. To many young men and women it is a practical and beneficial application of a sport they enjoy.

Oysters have enemies in the fish world, also. Two in particular, the salt-water drum fish and the ray, can devastate a bed of oysters. A salt-water drum fish, weighing as much as fifty to sixty pounds, has well-developed teeth set in a thick, broad, triangular bone structure located in the throat. A large school of these predators has been known to destroy a bedding ground in a single night. Drum fish are prevalent in the warm Gulf waters, and oystermen there must protect their bedding grounds by surrounding them with underwater fences of galvanized wire mesh strong enough to keep out the large fish.

The ray is a fish distinguished by two large fins extending from the sides of its flattened body. The fins are so large that this fish is almost as broad as it is long. The whiplike tail is used as a rudder. The several species of rays that attack oyster beds may attain lengths of four or five feet and weigh a hundred pounds or more. They are bottom feeders, having strong jaws and heavy, flat teeth which crush and grind the shells. One ray can easily destroy several acres of oysters within a short time. Lines of stakes are erected around oyster beds on the West Coast of the United States where rays are a major pest to keep this predator out. The French oyster grounds on the Biscay coast are similarly surrounded by palisades as protection against rays. Also, oystermen fish for these strange-looking creatures, drag the bottom of bays with trawl nets to catch them, and set out baited traps to entice them to enter.

Oysters are attacked by innumerable other sea creatures such as crabs, which nibble away at the margin of the shells until they can feed on the flesh. Also, crabs scurrying along the bottoms of oyster beds can stir up muddy sediment which can suffocate oysters. Various species of crabs in all waters of the world are fished not only to protect the valuable oyster beds but also to provide a delicious sweet-fleshed meat to humans. Blue, stone, and Dungeness crabs are delicacies that command a good

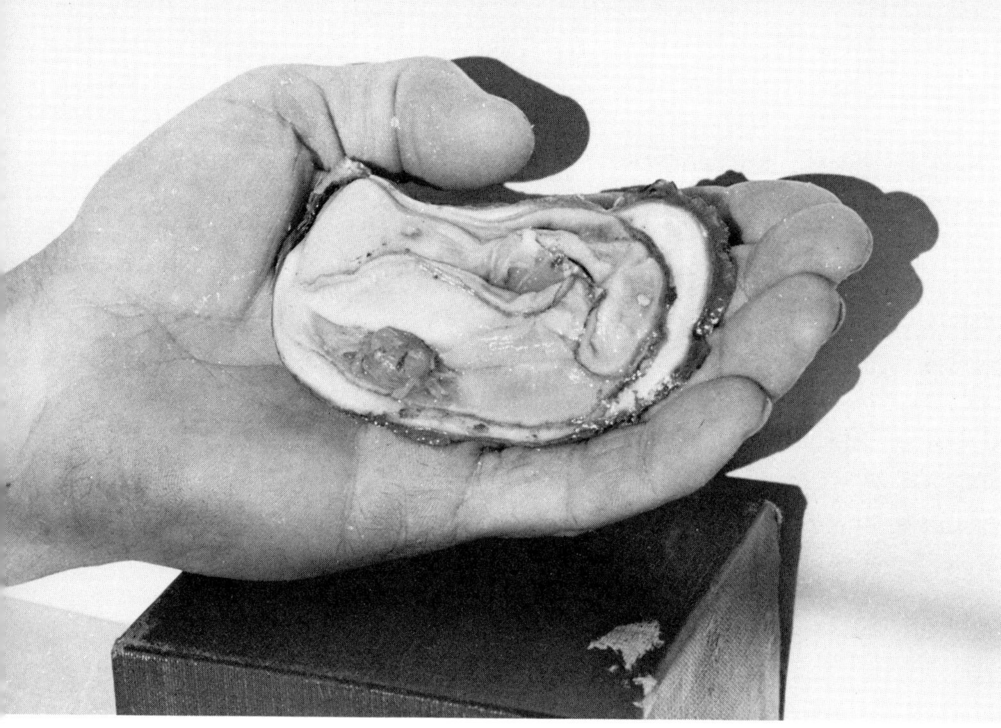

Notice the pea crab in lower left section of the oyster. This tiny sea creature eats food that otherwise would be assimilated by the oyster to produce healthy shell growth.

Courtesy of the
Virginia Institute of Marine Science

price at the market.

Most other crabs destructive to the oysters are of no value to man. An extremely tiny crab, one of the many species of pea crabs, was originally described by the Greek philosopher Aristotle before the birth of Christ. This minute crustacean has become known as the oyster crab. It lives inside the oyster's shells on the gills, picking off food, doing damage to the tissues, and thereby affecting the efficiency of the

38

assimilation of food by the oyster. This retards the normal development of an oyster, stunting its growth or even killing the mollusk. Often an oyster is host to many of these crabs at one time.

Another member of the oyster's family, the mussel, which is also a bivalve, can destroy an oyster bed rapidly. Mussels reproduce in even greater numbers than oysters and consume more food. Also, they attach themselves to oysters, growing in huge clumps or colonies which eventually smother the oysters.

There are sea worms and boring sponges of several species throughout the world which do not feed upon the oyster's flesh but attack its valves. Both the worms and sponges erode and disfigure oyster shells, making them unattractive to the buyer

A boring sponge growing on an oyster's shell — growth which eventually weakens and softens the oyster shell while making the mollusk's flesh thin and watery.

for the oyster-on-the-half-shell market. As these pests perforate and destroy shells, they also interfere with the fattening of the enclosed oysters which must then direct all their energies to the process of providing new shell growth.

The oyster is able to live out of water for considerable periods by contraction of the adductor muscle which shuts the valves like a vise. In its airtight shell, the animal so reduces its body functions that it can obtain the oxygen it requires from the sea water retained within its valves. This gives the creatures a defense against enemies and unfavorable conditions. It also makes it possible to hold oysters out of water for purposes of pest-control treatments, transplanting, shipping, or marketing without injuring them.

Many oysters infested with worms and boring sponges can be saved by immersion into a concentrated brine solution for a few minutes every two weeks or so, followed by exposure to the air. The oysters are then placed back in their beds. This process helps keep the shells free of the pests without injuring the oysters.

A number of microparasites are capable of greatly reducing the oyster population. However, they do not render oysters unfit for human consumption since humans are completely unaffected by them. Probably the most damaging is a water-borne parasitic fungus organism scientifically known as *Dermocystidium marinum,* called "Dermo" for short. This fungus was first noted in the 1940's in the Gulf of Mexico. Later it was identified in the oyster-rich waters of Chesapeake Bay. Dermo is especially prevalent in high salinity waters and causes high mortality during summer months. Control of the parasite is accomplished by transplanting oysters, before the arrival of the warm summer months, to waters of low salinity.

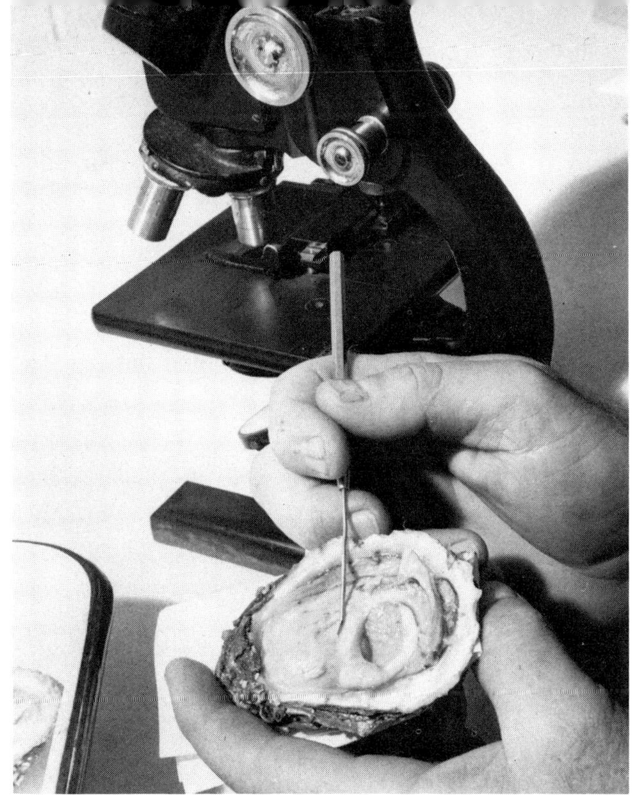

Marine scientist determining whether an oyster is host to a disease organism

Another organism causing heavy loss of oysters was discovered in the late 1950's. "MSX" was the term used for this parasite and simply stood for what scientists saw under the microscope—M standing for multi-nucleated, S indicating spheres, and X meaning unknown. Further study identified the organism as a protozoan, or one-celled animal, and it was scientifically named *Minchinia nelsoni;* yet its old name "MSX" persists. As with most diseases of oysters, waters of low salinity discourage the presence of these parasites.

41

Other sea and shore creatures also eat oysters. Among them are the frolicsome sea otter, that curious nocturnal land animal the raccoon, and a shore bird with a long slender bill commonly known as the oyster catcher. Although these animals may be classified as predators, they do not devastate entire oyster beds.

In addition to its many living enemies, there are numerous physical conditions which may be harmful to the oyster. Too much or too little fresh water has a damaging effect on the beds. Sudden changes in salinity cause shock to the oyster and death can result. Too high a degree of salinity brings forth an array of predators and diseases to attack the oysters. Serious losses can occur when gales churn the bottom mud, causing it to shift and smother a thriving bed. Hurricanes and storms pour forth huge amounts of rainfall over oyster beds and on the surrounding land. Swollen rivers and streams empty their flooded banks into bays, inlets, and estuaries, causing destruction to entire populations of these valuable mollusks.

Heat and cold are factors in many areas. If oysters are exposed above water between tides during very cold weather, they may be injured or killed. Water which is constantly above the 90°F mark is not good for oyster growth, and if a steady temperature of over 100°F is maintained the shelled animals will soon die.

The Red Tide, which occurs occasionally in many maritime areas of the world, renders oysters unfit for human consumption. Red Tide is caused by the extremely rapid reproduction of countless billions of microscopic organisms. These enormous populations are stimulated by the chemical richness of large amounts of river water delivered to the sea.

The organism produces a powerful poison that kills fishes, so that, when an outbreak of Red Tide occurs, beaches of extended sections of the coast are choked with the littered dead.

Oysters in Red Tide waters ingest the organisms, but no harm is done to the mollusks. However, when eaten, oysters from Red Tide waters cause severe reactions. Nausea, blurred vision, weakness, and a general feeling of sickness beset the human who feeds upon them. Death can even occur. When an infrequent outbreak of Red Tide takes place, harvesting of the oyster beds is stopped until all water samples are negative and the animals are free of the toxin.

Pollution by man with his ever increasing development of the waterfront has probably destroyed more rich oyster beds than all the predators and forces of nature combined. Areas that once were major suppliers of these succulent bivalves are either closed or else the oyster has been completely killed off.

Oysters from moderately polluted areas can be purified by placing them in chlorinated water for a time and then putting them back in non-polluted beds. But this is not the answer to the problem. Pollution must be curtailed.

It is in this area particularly that human endeavor must be directed if we are to sustain, enrich, and feed the peoples of the world. What an outrageous crime it would be if future generations were unable to eat any sea life due to human ignorance, indifference, or greed. Pollution is something that humans created and must control so as not to upset the roles that various creatures act out in the sea waters of the world.

A modern day oyster mound being formed
with the aid of machinery. Ancient mounds
were formed by man who discarded oyster
shells as he used them.

5. Oysters in History

The Roman historian, politician, and author Sallust wrote the above quote in 50 B.C. Roman soldiers who invaded the island of Britain discovered that the waters offered a plentiful supply of oysters. Desiring a steady supply of easily obtainable food, they set up their camps near the shoreline. As ships traveled back and forth from Rome to Britain, many Romans shipped oysters packed in bags of ice and snow back to their country. Here they were enjoyed at banquets by the rich and famous.

During these years many Roman homes installed large sea-water tanks where oysters were kept fresh for the table. The oyster became so highly prized that during the reign of Emperor Diocletian (A.D. 284-305) the Roman monetary unit, the denarius, was equal to the value of one oyster.

In the prehistoric dawn of man, oysters had been among the most common of animals in shallow, sheltered waters of bays, creeks, and estuaries. Being visible, especially at low tide, it was natural that primitive men entered the water and gathered up the mollusks. A thin stone or shell enabled the hunters to pry open the valves to taste the meat inside. Many years later, Jonathan Swift (1667-1745), brilliant English writer and author of *Gulliver's Travels,* is said to have stated that it was a bold man who first ate an oyster. Perhaps it was, but it was a fortunate man.

Huge and ancient mounds of oyster and other shells found near coasts around the world are evidence that oysters and other bivalves were a major food of primitive man. These mounds are so enormous that it took centuries for them to accumulate. In Europe, shell mounds have been unearthed in Denmark, Ireland, France, and Greece. The mound discovered in France is on the west coast in a locality named Brittany. It is made up of oyster, scallop, and mussel shells piled up fifteen yards above the marshland and is over seven hundred yards long by three hundred yards wide. Picture seven football fields end to end and three football fields side by side, filled with shells to a depth of seventy-five feet for an idea of the extent of this mound.

Off the coast of Asia in the Pacific Ocean waters, Japan and Australia have uncovered great mounds of shells. One such in New South Wales, Australia, was estimated to be hundreds of yards in length and several feet deep and wide.

In America, the coastal Indians, who like the Romans based their currency on shellfish, using dried or smoked oysters for trade or barter with inland tribes, were feasting on oysters more than four thousand years ago. This is proven by the tremendous piles of oyster shells found along the coasts. The largest shell mound discovered is at Damariscotta, Maine. It is estimated to contain seven million bushels of shells. At today's market price for oysters, this would net approximately 150 million dollars.

An article by T.C. Nelson, "The Boylston Street Fishweir," stated in 1942 that under that busy street in the heart of Boston a huge oyster bed had been unearthed and was considered to be over three thousand years old. Scientists are able to tell the age of a shell by carbon tests.

When the early colonists came to America, they were amazed at the number of oysters in the waters of this new land. According to historical records, in 1607 a group of settlers landed at Cape Henry, which was later to become part of the state of Virginia. Here they came upon a band of Indians. George Percy described

Above: These oyster shell fossils in sandstone matrix were used in the construction of a fireplace by the discoverer of the marine sediment on Tapo Mountain. *Right:* Oyster shell mining operations at Tapo Mountain, near Santa Susana, California.

Both photos: Wide World Photos

the incident, stating: "We came to a place where they (Indians) had made a great fire, and had been newly roasting oysters. When they perceived our coming, they fled away to the mountains and left many of the oysters in the fire. We ate some of the oysters, which were very large and delicate in taste." Later, in 1671, Arnoldus Montanus, in describing the advantages of the new land for early settlers, wrote: "Oysters, some a foot long, containing pearls, but few of brown color, were to be found in all waters of the Colony." Early settlers obviously believed the supply of oysters was inexhaustible, harvesting them not only for food but as fertilizer for crops.

People who settled in what today is Maryland complained to British authorities in 1680 "that their supplies of provisions becoming exhausted, it was necessary for them, in order to keep from starvation, to eat the oysters taken from along their shores." Not all people enjoyed the mollusk, and the oyster was not everyone's "pearl." As William Thackery, British novelist, stated: "I was never much of an oyster eater, nor can I relish them *in naturalibus* as some do, but require a quantity of sauces— lemons, cayenne peppers, bread and butter, and so forth, to render them palatable."

It is interesting to note that today the waters of Maryland are one of the richest oyster-producing areas in the world. But as the population increased, more and more oysters were being consumed. Within two hundred years, the natural beds of Maine and New Hampshire along the East Coast of the United States had been so intensely harvested that they were almost depleted. Today, except for a small area in Canada, there are few oysters north of Boston, Massachusetts.

The state of Louisiana, which borders on the Gulf of Mexico, also ranks as one

 Oysters Rockefeller — the gour-
met's delight!

Long Island Oyster Farms, Inc.

of the world's most productive areas. The historian Du Pratz, who spent sixteen years gathering material for his *Historie de la Louisiane,* published in 1734, told of the abundance and excellence of the oysters he found along the coastline and in the bayous. It was the Louisiana oyster that was first served up as Oysters Rocke-feller, a dish prepared with such rich ingredients that it was named after John D.

Rockefeller, the richest man in the world, by the French chef in New Orleans who created it.

On the West Coast of the United States, the finding of gold at Sutter's Mill in 1848 helped deplete the native oyster, *Ostrea lurida,* found in the waters off San Francisco. Enormous beds of *Ostrea* were ravaged to supply the appetites of men seeking to find their fortunes in gold. During this period, a plate of half a dozen oysters in San Francisco brought a price of twenty dollars, or two dollars an oyster. If one couldn't find gold in the earth, there was "gold" in harvesting oysters.

In 1859, a writer stated in a publication entitled *American Institute* that, in the city of New York, more money was spent for oysters than for butchers' meat. In 1865, the people of New York City, less than 900,000 inhabitants, consumed seven million bushels of oysters.

To great numbers of people, eating oysters has provided intense pleasure. Food from the sea since the earliest days has been associated with romance. Perhaps one reason for this thought's recurrence throughout the history of man is the Greek myth that Aphrodite, goddess of love, was born from the foam of the sea. Oysters are the most famous of all aquatic love food. The Roman poet Juvenal wrote that a woman "who deep mid-night on oyster sups" was regarded as immoral. Casanova, considered the greatest of lovers, kept oysters in his sea-filled bathtub, usually gulping down a hundred or so for breakfast. In his *Memoirs,* Casanova pronounced them "a spur to the spirit and to love." Even today the thought is present in the slogan of the Oyster Institute of America—"Eat Oysters, Love Longer."

6. A Creature Changed

Oysters were one of the earliest animals to be transported from one area to another and cultivated as food. This tasty bivalve which lies on its left side on the floor of the sea without any means of locomotion has probably traveled farther than any other sedentary animal.

The ancient world, while knowing nothing about the reproduction of oysters, knew much about the conditions necessary for their growth. Aristotle (384-322 B.C.) in his work *Historia Animalium,* stated that oysters attached themselves to broken pots tossed overboard by Greek sailors in the Mediterranean Sea. Aristotle wrote nothing about eating oysters. But the Romans, as we have seen, quickly discovered the food value and pleasure of eating oysters. Seneca, Roman philosopher, statesman, and playwright, wrote, "Oyster, dear to the gourmet, exciting rather than sating, all stomachs digest you, all stomachs bless you."

Pliny the Elder, in his work *Natural History*, noted that oysters discharged a milky, impregnating fluid. He also recorded the first attempt at oyster culture in Europe,

More than a thousand years after Aristotle's observation of "setting" oysters, man has applied this knowledge to ensure their supply.

U.S. Department of Commerce
National Marine Fisheries Service

Today's version of Sergius Orata's successful venture in raising oysters in man-made water enclosures

stating that a Sergius Orata in 95 B.C. successfully cultivated oysters in a secluded area near Naples.

Orata's methods consisted of preparing the grounds by removing other forms of marine life, planting "seed" or baby oysters, cultivating the growing oysters by keeping them separated so they could develop to a well-formed, mature size, and finally harvesting them when ready for market.

Sergius Orata, a good businessman, convinced the Romans that the cultivated oysters he raised had a superior taste. Soon he was making a profit and, in his enthusiasm, he spread out onto other people's property. A legal suit was brought against him by his neighbors as a result.

Pliny states that Orata started his artificial oyster beds "not for the gratification of gluttony, but of avarice, as he contrived to make a large income by this exercise of his ingenuity." Whatever Sergius Orata's motives were, he did prove that oysters could be cultivated artificially, and that they could be moved from one area to another. He is the first recorded advocate of oyster culture.

For approximately fifteen hundred years following the decline of the Roman Empire, people continued to feed upon the oyster, but there is little evidence that man cultivated the mollusk. There was no need of cultivation because there was little transportation to inland villages and towns, and the natural oyster beds easily fed the population along the coasts.

But as the population of the world increased, interest in the oyster reappeared. That master of the English language, William Shakespeare (1564-1616), referred to oysters in many of his plays. In *King Lear*, the court "Fool" asks the King, "Canst tell how an oyster makes his shell?" People in the arts, and working men and women, began to appreciate and extol the pleasures of eating oysters.

The cultivation of oysters in parks of water in England is believed to have started in the late seventeenth and early eighteenth centuries. Britons continued the Roman practice of raising oysters away from their natural beds in areas where food was plentiful so they could fatten quickly. During this period, records show that taxes were placed on underwater lands used for oyster cultivation in England.

In 1855 there was a major step forward in oyster culture. The oystermen of the

then unpolluted East River in New York discovered that spat settled on shells scattered over oyster beds during the spawning season. Using this knowledge, the men started the practice of scattering oyster shells over a bed. The State of New York passed a law in 1855 to secure to private farmers the rewards of their labor, and oyster culture was recognized by law.

This discovery in the East River took place three years before Coste, a French scientist known as the father of modern oyster culture, presented the same information to the Emperor Napoleon III.

During the closing years of the nineteenth century, oysters from the rich beds in Chesapeake Bay were transplanted to the increasingly exhausted northern beds. Chesapeake Bay, from the earliest days of colonization to the present, has been one of the mainstays of oyster production and cultivation.

Dredging for oysters in 1855, New York harbor

Long Island Oyster Farms, Inc.

A few years later, in an attempt to supplement the dwindling supply of the native oyster, *Ostrea lurida,* on the West Coast of the United States, the possibility of transplanting oysters from Japan was first discussed. Bashford Dean, a marine biologist who worked for the United States Fish and Wildlife Service, had been sent in 1890 on a journey to Europe which, although impressive, had no effect on American oyster culture. Later he went to Japan to observe the Japanese oyster culture. This trip brought results. In Asia, *Crassostrea gigas* was and is the most important commercial oyster. Its typically elongated shells may attain lengths of a foot or more. This species grows in profusion in the waters of Japan and Korea. Early attempts to establish

Japanese woman bringing in seed oysters to be shipped to the United States where they will be planted on the West Coast

United Press International

Crassostrea gigas, the Japanese oyster, on the American Pacific Coast in the years before World War I (1914-1918) met with little success, as most of the adult oysters died during the journey. However, in 1919, one shipment, believed dead, was dumped overboard in shallow water on American shores. A few years later a flourishing bed due to growth of spat which had attached to the dead oyster shells was found.

Obviously, all the oysters dumped into the water had not been dead.

Crassostrea gigas grew as well in American waters as in Japanese waters. However, they seldom spawned, so, each year, carefully selected, fairly mature seed was imported from Japan to achieve full maturity on the western coast of the United States and Canada. Due to a whim of nature during World War II, when Japan and the United States were at war with each other, unusually high temperatures induced spawning, and successful spat falls maintained the industry during these years.

Today, West Coast states are once again dependent upon imported seed oysters from Japan. The great Pacific oyster, as it is known in America, is the main source of supply on the West Coast. This important industry brings in millions of dollars annually to oyster farmers in California and Washington. This importation of Japanese seed oysters is another example of oysters being raised and harvested in artificial beds, normally not present but made by man. Usually, such beds do not spawn and reproduce in colder waters.

In Europe where the flat oyster, *Ostrea edulis*, was the most important commercial oyster for centuries, a similar situation developed a number of years before the American experiment with the Japanese oyster. In 1868, *Crassostrea angulata*, the Portuguese oyster which occurs along the east and south coasts of Portugal and Spain, was imported into France to supplement the sparse native supply of *Ostrea edulis*. Today, the Portuguese oyster forms large natural beds in the southern waters of France. It has since been transplanted to Britain, where it grows well but seldom spawns due to the low water temperature. However, there have been times, although quite infrequently, during hot summers that spawning took place and spat settled and grew.

Britain originally had the greatest producing *Ostrea edulis* beds in Europe. However, due to over-fishing, pollution, and other environmental factors, native oyster production declined. The Portuguese oysters transplanted from natural beds aided greatly in increasing the productivity of many oyster-producing nations in Europe.

In France there are numerous cultivated beds. The French especially prize oysters with green gills. These are the result of water with a rather high temperature and high salinity, and an abundance of certain long, spindle-shaped diatoms. Diatoms are the microscopic plant life which make up approximately six-tenths of the plankton, small plant and animal life, of the sea. Diatoms sometimes are called the meadow grass of the sea. Being extremely practical people, the French take little chance with nature and annually place their marketable oysters in man-made beds, known as parks. The exact time to bed the oysters is decided by scientists who carefully test the parks for the perfect water conditions. Within a few days the oysters absorb the chlorophyll produced by the diatoms and the greening of the gills takes place. This delight of the French gourmet is shipped to market to be enjoyed by many.

The French were early innovators in breeding oysters and hit upon the idea of using half-cylinder roofing tiles, coated with lime, as collectors for the young oyster larvae. The spat readily attach themselves to the tiles during the summer months. The tiles are carefully tended, and young oysters are transplanted to parks where they fatten on the plentiful supply of food provided by nature.

In the northern waters of the United States and Canada, where the native beds of *Crassostrea virginica* were largely depleted many years ago, attempts have been made to introduce *Ostrea edulis* from Europe. The cold waters, it was believed, might provide a suitable home for the European flat oyster which has a lower breeding temperature. Initial attempts were quite successful, especially in Boothbay Harbor, Maine, where three thousand European oysters were planted. In a period of three years it was noted that the original oysters had grown well, while young oysters had settled on rocks and other material in the bay area. Scientifically, the venture was a success, but commercially it had little or no effect on re-establishing an oyster industry in this area of North America.

Today, two of the most industrialized nations in the world, the United States and Japan, support the most modern and important oyster industries.

During the long years man has known and appreciated the oyster, many artificial beds have been created. The oyster has been moved from one section of a country's shore to another, from one continent's to another, where the oyster would not naturally have settled. Although the new areas, in some cases, were unsuitable for larvae, they were perfect for the successful growth of adult oysters. Today, man is still transplanting oysters from their natural beds to other man-made beds in areas where there is a better supply of food and no pollution.

So the practice that started with the Romans is still carried on today. The oyster, silent, without locomotion, has had its home changed many times. Some whimsical writers have tried to show how the oyster might feel about all this moving around.

The brilliant British author, Lewis Carroll, perhaps best described the oyster's reaction in *Through the Looking Glass*:

> The eldest Oyster winked his eye,
> And shook his heavy head—
> Meaning to say he did not choose
> To leave the oyster bed.

Edward Lear, in one of his *Nonsense Alphabets*, probably made the most plaintive appeal for an oyster as it faces the powerful forces of nature and man:

O

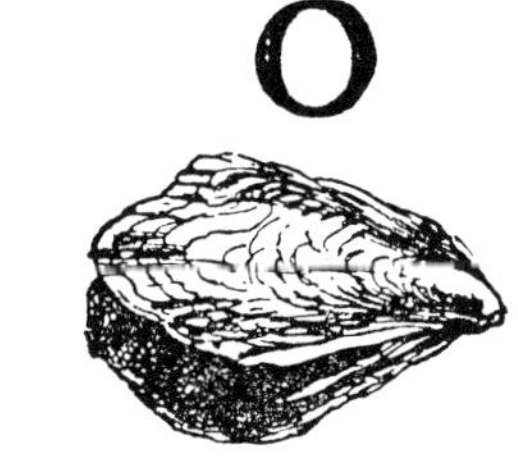

O was an oyster,
Who lived in his shell:
If you let him alone,
He felt perfectly well.

O

Open-mouthed oyster!

Left: Oysterman harvesting his "tonged" catch. Note the nail-like teeth in lower right corner that scrape the bottom of the sea, scratching up the mollusks as the oysterman works his scissor-like tongs from a boat.

United Press International

Below: Hosing the cultch overboard to form a floor or bed for young oyster seed

U.S. Department of Commerce
National Marine Fisheries Service

7. Cultivating and Harvesting Oysters

In America, a number of oystermen reap the harvest of natural beds. The oysters are native to the water where they live, and spawning, reproduction, and growth are left to nature. But man sets up laws regulating harvesting.

Harvesting of these beds, owned by the state and open to the public, is done mainly by tongs. Tongs are two hinged wooden poles measuring up to twenty-six feet in length. At the end of the scissor-like tongs are two baskets armed with teeth. The oysterman, standing in his boat, places the tongs into the water until they reach the bottom. Then he works them like a pair of shears, pushing the handles together, causing the teeth to scoop the oysters into the basket. The tongs are then brought up from the sea and the catch placed in the boat.

Numerous natural beds have disappeared due to over-fishing or environmental factors, such as pollution. So, many oystermen became farmers. Essentially, the basic methods are similar to the techniques used by the Romans. Improvements in preparation of the ground, seed planting, cultivation, and harvesting are the result of increased knowledge plus better equipment.

Oystermen in many sections of the United States lease land from the state. Most states also charge rent based on the number of acres farmed. The leased land may have a natural bed of oysters. If so, the farmer usually only cultivates and harvests oysters, and may move the oysters to other beds to attain maturity and acquire the salty flesh that the consumer desires. If the farmer has land where spawning and setting is good but growth slow, he may produce seed oysters. These are sold to farmers whose ground does not produce young oysters.

Many leased lands do not have a natural bed. Then the farmer studies the conditions of the bottom. The best oyster bottoms are those which are stable. Oysters planted on sand may be rolled around and shifted. Those planted in muddy bottoms may become buried or covered over by silt. These grounds are not productive. After selection of a suitable bottom, the first step is to attempt to remove marine life that may be harmful to oysters. Secondly, in most farms, material known as cultch is spread over the bottom. Tiles, gravel, finely broken building blocks, branches, and other material are used. Oyster and clam shells are the most common and effective cultch. These shells provide a floor for seed oysters to rest on. Cultch is deposited before the peak spawning season so larvae have a clean, firm surface to "strike" or set on. This greatly increases the productivity of the farm.

Cultch shells are loaded on a boat that has a wide deck, high sides, and shallow

A dredgful of approximately ten bushels
of oysters about to be hoisted aboard

Long Island Oyster Farms, Inc.

draft so that the craft may go into shallow water. The deck holds many shells while
the high sides keep them from falling off in rough water. Some oystermen pull a
barge loaded with shells. These are evenly spread on the bottom so that over-crowding
or clustering of oysters is lessened. This aids in developing a good quality market
oyster.

The farmer then turns his energies to collecting seed oysters for the bed. These
oysters, approximately one inch in size, are scattered over the leased area where,
hopefully, they rest on the cultch. Some farmers pull a spike-toothed harrow (similar

to a huge rake) over their grounds after planting to distribute the seed more evenly.

The young oysters may reach maturity on these grounds. Harvesting may be done by tonging or dredging. Some farmers use tongs if the cultch is thin, has sunk, or shifted. They believe tongs are less damaging to the beds than dredges. The more modern and efficient method is the use of dredges. A dredge has a metal box-like frame usually measuring five or six feet in width. Located at the front of the box is a convex blade which helps to loosen the oysters from the bed. The box serves as a scraper. Attached to the box is a strong metal bag or pouch which may scoop a thousand or more oysters from the bottom in a short time. In reality the word "scrape" is a more accurate expression than dredge. Scraped, or dredged, oysters are seldom sorted or culled by the farmer to remove empty shells, undersized oysters, or debris. When these oysters are sold they are culled at the market by the buyer and the price paid is based on the number of good marketable oysters per bushel of unloaded material. Tonged oysters are always culled by the farmer and the small oysters are returned to the water, hopefully to rebed.

In many farms oysters do not achieve maturity in their first bed. These oysters are usually moved after a year on the original bed. This period varies with the climate and other environmental factors of each region. They may be gathered to be trans-planted either by tonging or dredging. Placed on a boat, the oysters are taken, in many instances, to their final bed, usually in waters high in salinity. Some farmers move their oysters several times before they reach the market. It is in the final bed that oysters, due to the high degree of saline water which they feed upon, obtain the delicious and salty flavor that is appreciated by oyster eaters. The final harvest

Unloading a "catch" at the market

U.S. Department of Commerce
National Marine Fisheries Service

is usually done by dredging and the oysters are sold to the market.

Some oyster farmers divide their acreage into plots. They usually have three plots—one for seed oysters, another for harvesting, and the third for oysters in several stages of growth. This allows continual farming of their grounds.

A number of oystermen purchase acreage around their farms in an effort to keep predators away. This area is left unseeded in the hope that natural enemies of the oyster will not travel across this stretch of underwater land to feed on the valuable mollusk.

A variation of bottom farming is the use of rafts or floats. Cultch, instead of being spread over an area, is strung like beads and suspended from the raft. It hangs in the water where oysters spawn. The larvae set on the shells. After a month, the strings of shells are pulled from the water and only the healthiest and largest young oysters are allowed to remain, while the others are scraped off. The cultch wires are returned to the water. At the end of the growing season, the crop is harvested by lifting the wires out of the sea and removing the now mature oysters. Because the bivalves are suspended in water and not lying on the bottom, many predators such as the oyster drill and the starfish are unable to feed on them. Cultivation by this method greatly increases the harvest. However, a major factor to be considered is the constant attention that the farmer must pay to his crop. Also, some oystermen contend that the more desired, rounder-shaped oyster is not produced in this fashion.

A most interesting and farsighted project is hatchery rearing of oysters. This is a scientific breakthrough in aqua-culture in which man, in a laboratory setting, controls the birth and growth of the mollusk. A major reason for the success of this approach with oysters is the fact that they are sedentary, thus making them controllable.

In the hatchery, marine biologists studying every aspect of the life cycle of the oyster select certain specimens for their superior breeding qualities. These are parent oysters, male and female, and they are induced to spawn by the warming of the water in the breeding tanks.

Algae, having first been gathered in large vats scooped up from the sea, is grown in the hatchery. Scientists make every attempt to feed young oysters the proper diet for successful growth. Within twenty days the oyster has developed its foot appendage, and in natural surroundings it would attempt to attach itself to a suitable

Left: A scientist pushes cord through old oyster shell during an experiment in string culture. *Right:* Farmers checking growth of seed oysters in raft farming

object. In the hatchery, scientists have eliminated this stage and the young oysters settle on the bottom of the tanks. Here, they may be easily moved about by man so that they will develop the desirable round shell.

The developing oysters remain in the hatchery for a period of approximately six weeks. They are then placed on trays which have a fine screen covering the top and bottom, allowing free flow of water. The screen also prevents loss of the small shellfish. Trays of juvenile oysters are then placed in the hatchery nursery. This is

A modern day oyster farm. The building houses the hatchery while the water in the foreground is the nursery.

a body of secluded water which is free of predators and pollution. In this environment, mortality is almost zero.

One enterprising venture in hatchery oysters is being successfully carried out by the Long Island Oyster Farms. The nursery of this company is located in a small lagoon at the rear of the Long Island Lighting Company's generating plant. The lighting company pumps water in from Long Island Sound to cool the generators manufacturing electricity. The water becomes warm while cooling the machinery. It is discharged into the lagoon, where it warms the natural water to a minimum temperature of 40°F. This allows a year-round growing season for oysters. During the process, the water's only change is in temperature, and it is chemically pure.

In the nursery, the trays are regularly raised and the oysters cleaned and sorted

Right: The baby oysters in larval tanks are fed specially grown algae in a scientifically controlled environment, with emphasis on proper temperature and water purity. When ready, they are placed on screened trays which serve as cradles and lowered into the lagoon. *Below:* Baby oysters swimming in larval tanks in the safety of the hatchery have been produced from carefully selected parent oysters. *Below right:* Juvenile oysters are checked and cleaned at least once a week by a marine biologist. These tiny shellfish, about 8 to 10 weeks old, will be returned in the covered trays to the warm-water lagoon adjacent to the hatchery at the Long Island Oyster Farms for further growth before being transplanted to growing beds.

All photos: Long Island Oyster Farms, Inc.

according to size. After about six months, depending upon the time of the year, the young oysters are transplanted to beds in the open sea.

The hatchery method has reduced the normal growing period from four years to as low as two and a half years. When the oysters are ready to be harvested, they are scooped from the deep waters by oyster boats using dredges.

The constructive use of thermal pollution (warm water discharged from an industrial plant) plus the knowledge of marine biology has established a new industry. Long Island Sound waters which a few years ago were supplying oysters worth a million dollars to the public are now marketing about fifty million dollars worth of oysters. Acre for acre, oysters are one of the most valuable crops that can be cultivated. Shellfish account for about 46 per cent of the dollar value of today's total United States sea catch of approximately 500 million dollars.

Many people, including some marine scientists, believe that this method and others similar to it are the means of supplying man with much of the necessary protein for his diet. However, there are other scientists and environmentalists who are concerned that warm water discharged by power plants will upset the delicate balance of nature in the sea. All forms of marine life will probably grow faster, increase in number, and perhaps have a shorter life span. This is a question that has to be studied carefully and evaluated before an answer is forthcoming.

Hatchery experimentation is being carried on with other marine life such as clams, shrimp, lobster, and fish. Today, man no longer stands on the threshold of the age of aquaculture, he is deeply involved in it.

8. "Oysters R in Season"

"It is unseasonable and unwholesome in all months that have not an R in their name to eat an oyster." This ancient belief persists to this day. Doubtless it is due to the difficulty of keeping oysters fresh while transporting them in summer. True, during the R-less months oysters reproduce, which makes them lean and watery, but not harmful. There is nothing wrong with eating *Crassostrea* at any time, and *Ostrea* are distasteful only during their eight-day period of incubation. However, it is still a common sight to see fish stores advertising in September that "Oysters R in Season." This is a fallacy, a myth that modern refrigeration and rapid transportation should soon destroy once and for all.

After oysters are brought to the shore, they may be processed in different ways. Fairly large, well-formed oysters from waters that have imparted the perfection of taste are sold to the raw bar trade. These oysters command top prices. They are usually packed in burlap oyster bags or bushel baskets and tagged with the oysterman's permit number, date, and location of the bedding grounds. State health departments

Culling and sorting oysters at a processing plant. Notice the culling irons in the men's hands that are used to clear off any debris from the shells and also to separate attached oysters. The best formed oysters are selected for the raw bar trade.

Long Island Oyster Farms, Inc.

periodically check the beds and the oysters obtained from the beds to insure and maintain purity. These oysters are loaded into refrigerated trucks and shipped throughout the country to fish stores, oyster counters, and restaurants.

Oysters less perfect are sent to factories. These are usually shoveled direct from boats to conveyer belts which carry them into the factory where they are "shucked" (opened by hand) or placed in huge hoppers or kettles for steaming apart. When the shell is open, the meat is removed, washed, packed into cans or other containers, and shipped by refrigerated trucks to consumers.

Today, many oysters produced for the market are fairly small in comparison to those sold to the public fifty years ago. The major reason is that many oyster farmers harvest their crop as fast as they can to avoid losing it to predators, disease, and environmental factors. Also soup companies, since the advent of frozen soup, have demanded smaller oysters. This has greatly benefited the oyster farmer.

In recent years, flash-frozen raw oysters with a number of savory toppings have become available to people no matter where they live. And in stews and soups, fried,

To facilitate the opening or shucking of an oyster, it is helpful to have an ordinary pair of pliers and a professionally made oyster knife. A right-handed person usually holds an oyster in his left hand, while holding the knife in his right hand. The reverse is usually true for left-handed people. 1. Hold the oyster with its deeper-cupped, left valve in the palm of your hand with the flatter valve facing you. Clip a section of the oyster's bill with your pliers. 2. Holding the knife about ¼ inch from its point, enabling you to have better control, insert it carefully into the clipped bill. Work the knife in a circular fashion until you feel or see the valves separating. Remove the top shell. 3. Work the knife carefully around and underneath the oyster until you sever it from the bottom muscle which attaches it to the lower valve. Do not drain the liquid. The oyster, lying in its own juices, is now ready to eat.

Jan Cook

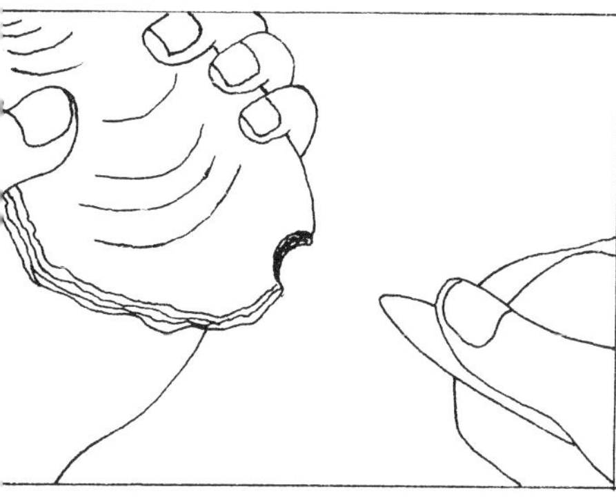

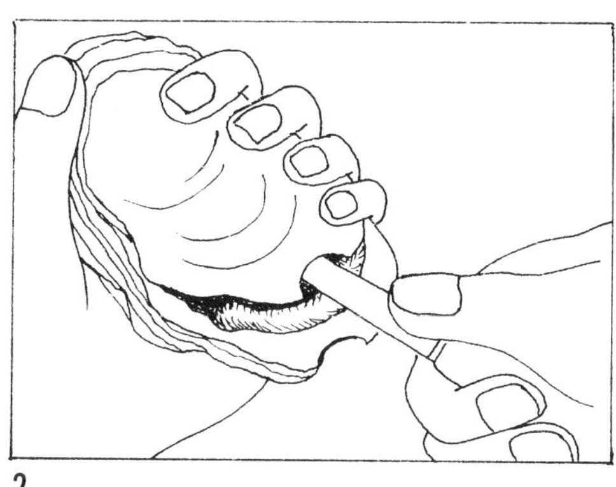

2

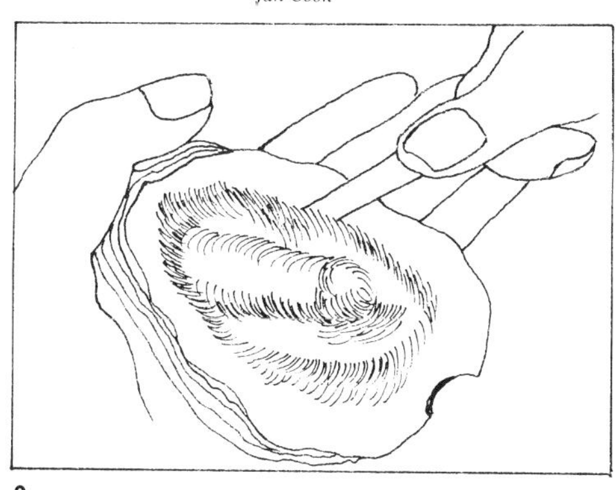

3

boiled, or baked, chefs and cooks the world over have devised tempting ways to present the oyster.

Perhaps the most primitive and satisfying way to eat oysters is raw, either shucking them yourself or having someone more experienced do it. Shucking an oyster is quite difficult for a novice. The oyster must always be held with the deeper, cupped valve in the palm of the hand, the flatter valve on top. With the tip of the oyster knife about a quarter inch from the point, carefully attempt to insert the blade between the valves. With experience, this becomes easier. After the tip has entered the valves, work the knife between them in a circular fashion. The top valve is then removed and the oyster with its juices will lie in the deeper lower valve.

There are two ways to eat raw oysters, by hand or with a fork. The former is simpler. Take the shell in your hand, put it to your lips, and gently slide the oyster into your mouth. Be extremely careful not to spill any of the juices. As the oyster enters your mouth, bite into the flesh with your teeth, thus obtaining more juices and the delicate taste of the oyster itself. Press it against the roof of your mouth with your tongue to obtain maximum taste before you let the salty flesh slip past your palate.

The more genteel method of eating an oyster is to use a fork. Then remaining juices are poured from the shell into your mouth. The choice is yours, but why bother with a tool when none is needed?

In many areas of the world, various condiments such as horseradish, ketchup, Tabasco, cayenne pepper, as well as lemon juice, oyster crackers, and innumerable

Oysters on the half shell

Long Island Oyster Farms, Inc.

other mixtures, are applied to the oyster before it is eaten. This adds to the delight for many; to others, the simple oyster resting in its own juices is the treasure. No other flavoring is needed or desired—the oyster is the king, or queen, as the case may be.

In the annals of oyster eating, it is reported that an Irishman named Dando, who weighed over two hundred pounds, ate half his weight of the mollusks in one day. He survived to live a long life, and when he died, his grave was encircled with oyster shells. The *Guinness Book of World Records* cites a Yorkshireman, Peter Jaconelli, who ate 500 of the bivalves in 48 minutes, 7 seconds, as the world's champion oyster eater. This amounts to the consumption of more than ten oysters per minute.

Perhaps writers have made more attempts to describe this highly prized mollusk than any other sea creature. Cyrano De Bergerac, French poet, soldier, and proud possessor of an extraordinarily large nose, said of an opened oyster in the early seventeenth century: "You have never seen the sea but in an oyster on the shell."

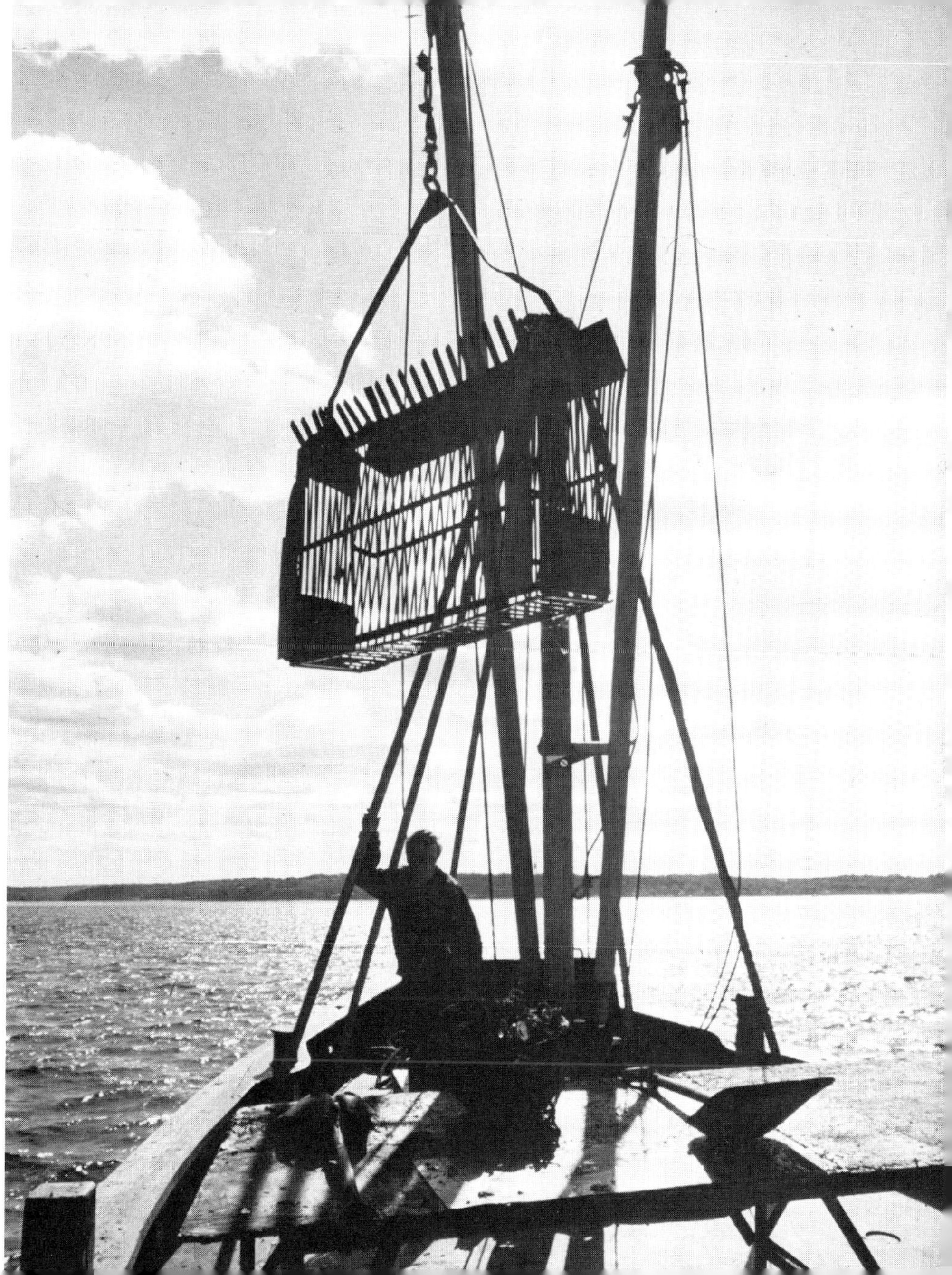

With empty dredge hanging from the spars, an oysterman heads out to harvest the delectable "king" or "queen" of the sea.
Long Island Oyster Farms, Inc.

SELECTED BIBLIOGRAPHY

Bailey, R. S., and Biggs, F. C. *Let's Be Oyster Farmers*. Virginia Institute of Marine Science and the School of Marine Science, College of William and Mary, 1968.

Barrett, Elinor M. *The California Oyster Industry*. Resources Agency of California Department of Fish & Game, Fish Bulletin 123, 1963.

Bolitho, Hector. *The Glorious Oyster*. New York: Horizon Press Inc., 1961.

Clark, Eleanor. *The Oysters of Locmariaquer*. New York: Pantheon Books, 1964.

DeGouy, Louis P. *The Oyster Book*. New York: Greenburg Publisher, 1951.

Ingle, R. M., and Whitfield, Jr., W. K. *Oyster Culture in Florida*. Florida Division of Salt Water Fisheries, Educational Series No. 5, 1968.

Long Island Oyster Farms, Incorporated. *Publications*. New York.

Matthiessen, George C. *A Review of Oyster Culture and the Oyster Industry in North America*. Massachusetts: Woods Hole Oceanographic Institution, n.d.

Tarter, V., revised by Westley, R.E. *Oyster Farming in Washington State*. Washington Department of Fisheries, 1971.

Waldo, E. *The Louisiana Oyster Story*. Louisiana Wild Life and Fisheries Commission, Wildlife Education Bulletin No. 32, 1962.

Yonge, C.M. *Oysters*. London: Collins, 1960.